It's Winter!

Acknowledgments
Executive Editor: Diane Sharpe
Supervising Editor: Stephanie Muller
Design Manager: Sharon Golden
Page Design: Ian Winton
Photography: Bruce Coleman: cover (top right, left, bottom right),
pages 9, 15, 19, 23, 25; Image Bank: cover (middle right); NHPA: pages 13, 17;
Tony Stone Worldwide: page 27; Alex Ramsay: page 21.

ISBN 0-8114-3707-8

It's Winter!

Michael Herschell

Illustrated by
Annabel Spenceley

STECK-VAUGHN
C O M P A N Y
ELEMENTARY • SECONDARY • ADULT • LIBRARY

On bright winter mornings,
the frost sparkles in the sun.

I can see my breath.

10

On cold winter days,
your breath looks white
when you breathe out.

11

During the winter, water freezes
and makes ice.

13

Many plants and trees rest in
the winter. But some trees and
bushes have berries then.

15

16

It is hard for birds to find food in the winter. They eat the berries on bushes.

18

It is nice to give birds extra
food to eat during the winter.

In the winter, there is not much grass for animals to eat. Farmers have to give their animals extra food.

21

During the cold winter weather, many small animals hibernate.

When snow covers the ground,
you can look for animal tracks.

Snowy weather is fun. You can do many different things.

These are some things we might see in the winter. Can you name them all?

Index